Cynthia

Thank you

THE LIFE AND JOURNEY OF ENAVED & NAVA

Written By Thomas DeVane
Illustrated By DeAndra Roy

Copyright © 2021 by Thomas DeVane

All rights reserved. No part of this publication may be reproduced or transmitted by any means, without prior permission of the publisher.

ISBN: 978-0-9705788-0-8

Published by Thomas DeVane

"Daddy, why does Mommy have a basketball in her stomach?"

"Oh son, Mommy doesn't have a basketball in her stomach. She has your little sister in there and tomorrow she's going to give birth."

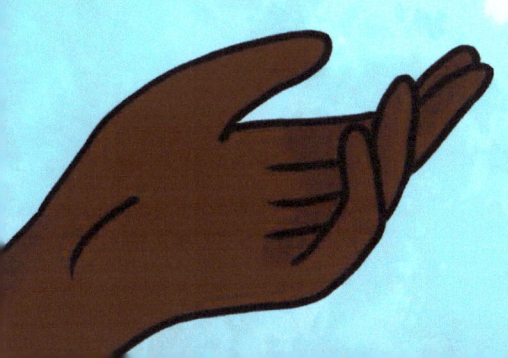

"Does that mean it's her birthday?"

"Yes, EnaVed, your sister's birthday will be the same day she comes into the world and looks at all the things you and I can see."

"That's why we call it a birthday."

"It's the day you were born. Once a year, on that day, we celebrate to acknowledge your special day of life, joy and giggles."

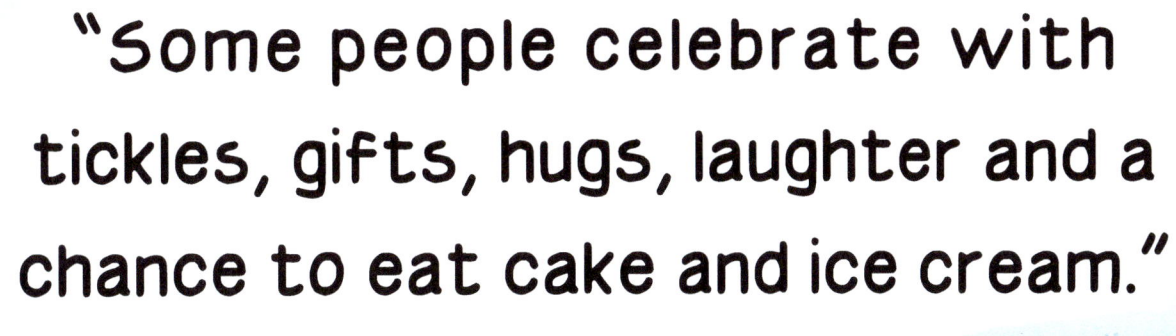

"Some people celebrate with tickles, gifts, hugs, laughter and a chance to eat cake and ice cream."

"Wake up, EnaVed, it's time to go."

EnaVed shakes his head asking, "Daddy, can I have one more minute," in a small little voice, still yawning.

"We're going to the hospital to see your baby sister."

Father and EnaVed arrive at the hospital. Mommy introduces Nava to her big brother.

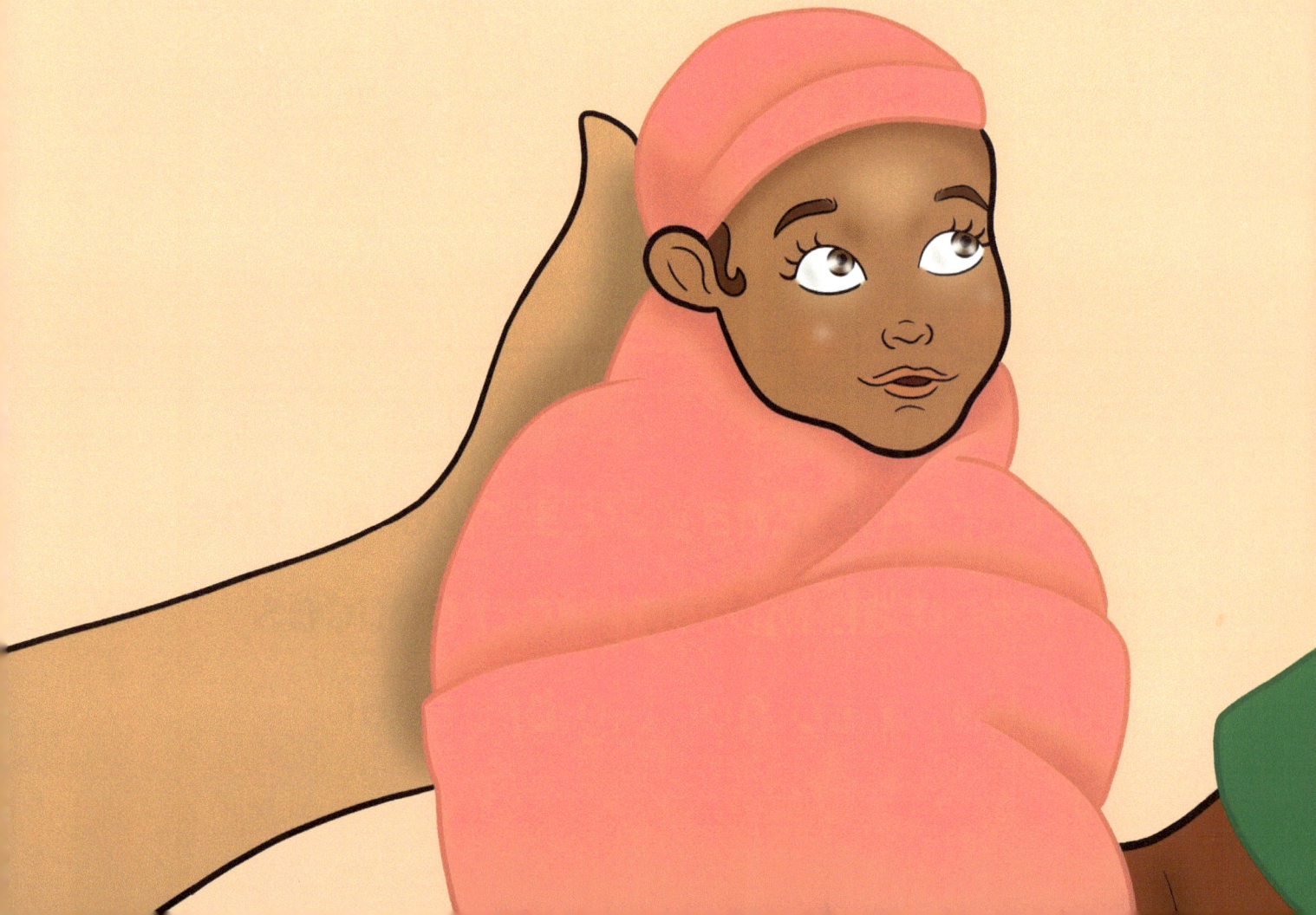

CPSIA information can be obtained
at www.ICGtesting.com
Printed in the USA
BVHW021157121121
621500BV00005B/28